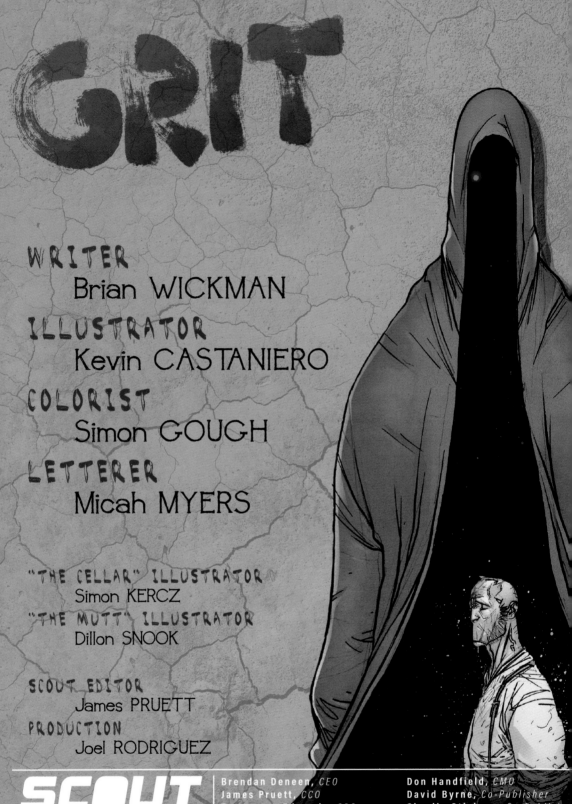

GRIT

WRITER
Brian WICKMAN

ILLUSTRATOR
Kevin CASTANIERO

COLORIST
Simon GOUGH

LETTERER
Micah MYERS

"THE CELLAR" ILLUSTRATOR
Simon KERCZ
"THE MUTT" ILLUSTRATOR
Dillon SNOOK

SCOUT EDITOR
James PRUETT
PRODUCTION
Joel RODRIGUEZ

SCOUT COMICS

Brendan Deneen, *CEO*
James Pruett, *CCO*
Tennessee Edwards, *CSO*
James Haick III, *President*

Don Handfield, *CMO*
David Byrne, *Co-Publisher*
Charlie Stickney, *Co-Publishe*
Joel Rodriguez, *Head of Desig*

FB/TW/IG:
@Scoutcomics

LEARN MORE AT:
www.scoutcomics.com

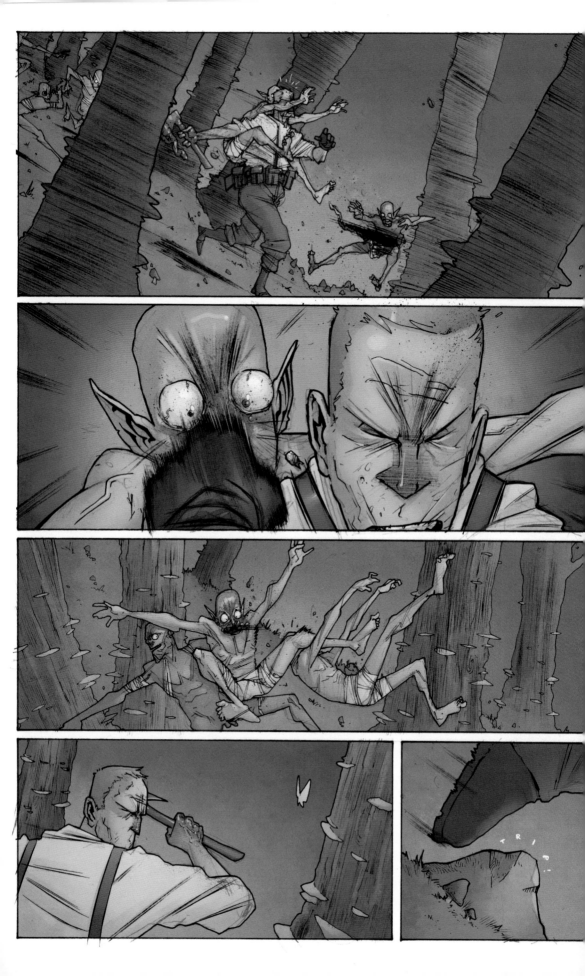

TERRIBLY RUDE OF YOU TO DROP IN UNINVITED, STRANGER...

...BUT I AM A **GRACIOUS** HOST, AND WILL FORGIVE YOU THAT DISCOURTESY. TELL ME, WHAT'S YOUR NAME?

NAME'S **BARROW**, AND--

NO, NO...

...PLEASE, TAKE A SEAT.

ORDINARILY, MY SERMONS ARE OPEN ONLY TO THE **TRULY** PIOUS...

...BUT MAYBE IT'S **DIVINE PROVIDENCE** THAT BROUGHT YOU HERE TONIGHT.

"OR COULD BE YOU'VE JUST GOT SHIT LUCK."

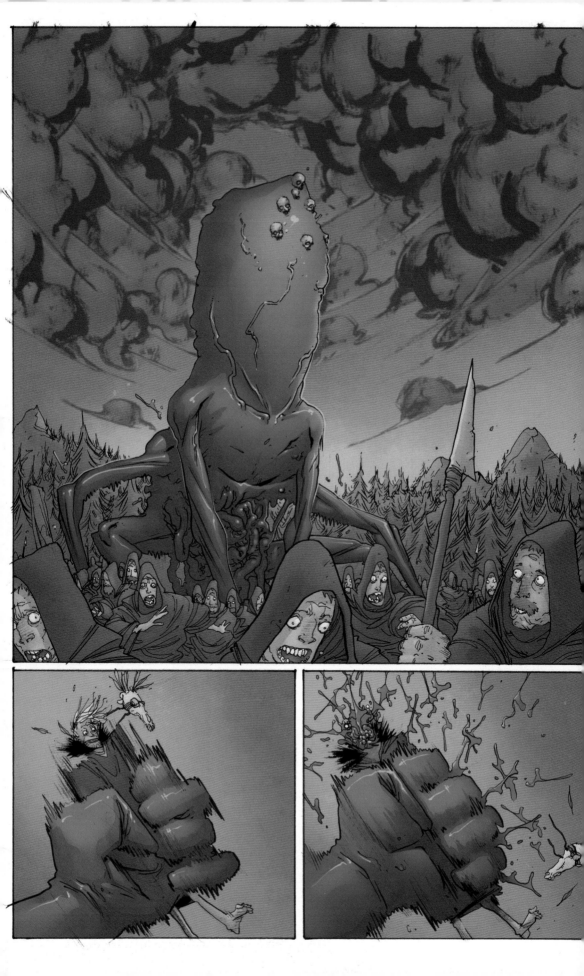

WELL--

--SHIT.

BOM!

"TROLL PROBLEM."

HMPH.

SSSSSS

sKREEEEE

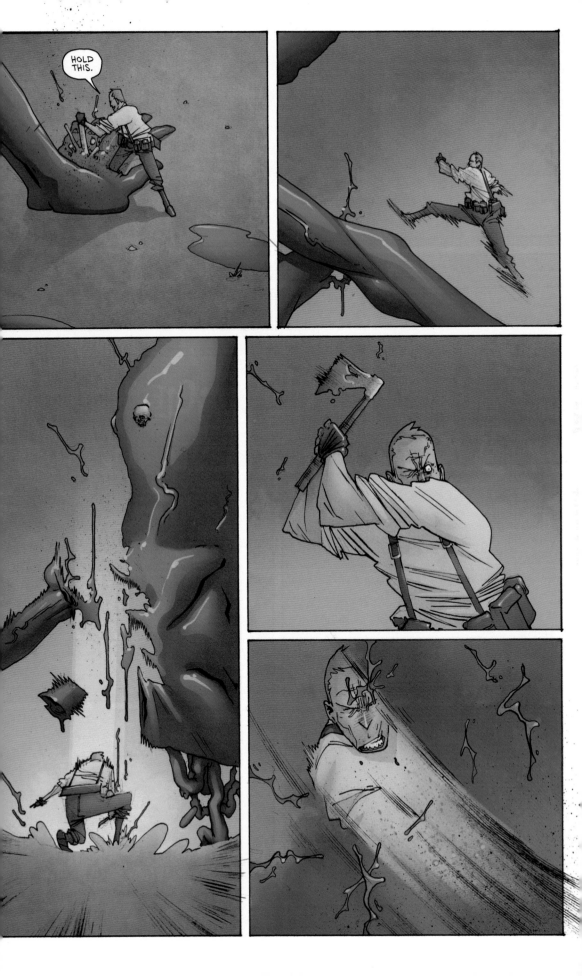

HAVE YOU LOST YOUR MIND?! YOU DON'T HIRE THE **ASHEN BASTARD** JUST CUS YOU'RE TOO CHEAP TO BUY MANURE.

HE AIN'T TO BE TRIFLED WITH!

AIN'T THE SAME SONG YOU WERE SINGING WHEN THAT REVENANT GOT ALL COZY IN YOUR CELLAR.

NOW THAT'S DIFFERENT AND YOU **KNOW** IT. DESPERATE TIMES AND SUCH.

MHM.

HE'S A **BARROW**, AND BARROWS ARE WICKED FOLK!

IF I MAY...

I KNOW MORE THAN MOST ABOUT HIS MA-- ABOUT THE **FOUL** THINGS SHE DONE--

--BUT HE AIN'T HIS MOTHER.

CHAPTER
TWO

THE BLOOD-SOAKED GROVE.

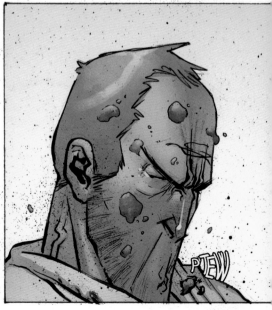

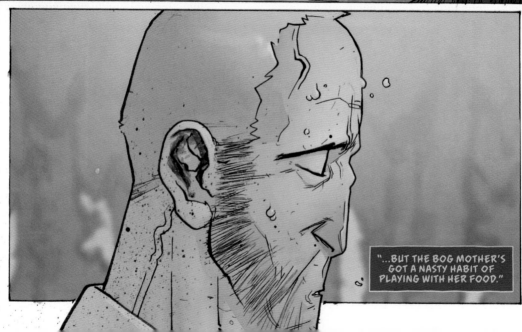

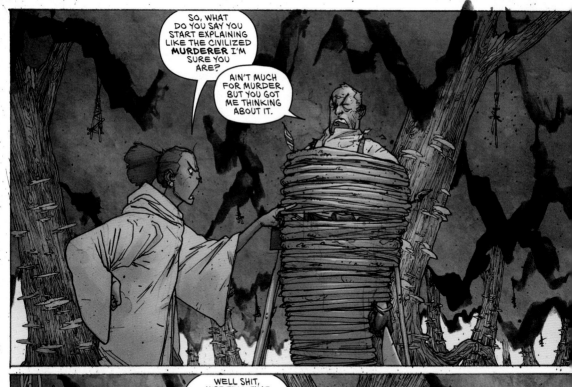

SO, WHAT DO YOU SAY YOU START EXPLAINING LIKE THE CIVILIZED **MURDERER** I'M SURE YOU ARE?

AIN'T MUCH FOR MURDER, BUT YOU GOT ME THINKING ABOUT IT.

WELL SHIT, JUST TELL THAT TO THE LITERAL **PILE OF BODIES** I FOUND. I'M **SURE** THEY'LL UNDERSTAND.

DIDN'T KILL NOBODY. COUPLE OF GOBLINS, SURE, BUT THEY CAME FOR ME.

BIG BLOOD THING DID THOSE OTHER FOLKS IN.

BIG BLOOD THING?

TALL AS THE TREES.

CLIMBED OUT OF SOME TROLL CORPSES OR SOMETHING.

I CHOPPED IT UP.

YOU WANNA LET ME GO NOW?

YOU **WHAT?**

CHAPTER THREE

RECKON THAT NICE GIRL AND HER GRANDPA ARE DOOMED, HUH?

YUP.

JUST WANT TO REMIND YOU THAT WE'RE DOING THIS **MY WAY**.

CUTTING IT UP DIDN'T WORK LAST TIME AND IT'S NOT GOING TO WORK TODAY.

GOT IT?

MHM.

I'M SERIOUS. YOU **CHOSE** TO TAG ALONG.

UH HUH. WE'RE HERE.

BLACK DOG BOTTOM

YOU JUST DON'T QUIT.

SOON ENOUGH, YOU TOO SHALL BEND TO THE WILL OF...

...GRACHIEL, ARCH-DEMON OF THE--

SPLAT

BLAM

THUD

WHAT THE--

SQUELCH

UH--

DON'T BOTHER.

NOTHING TO SAY.

YOU'RE EITHER TOO DUMB OR TOO STUBBORN TO REALIZE...

...MAYBE YOU **DON'T** ALWAYS KNOW BEST.

EITHER WAY...

...GUESS IT'S TRUE WHAT THEY SAY ABOUT OLD DOGS.

END

WHAT ARE YOU GOING TO DO?

KILL ME?

NO, I S'POSE NOT.

HM.

KREEEEEK

I KID, FRIEND, I'LL BE ON MY WAY.

THE BARKEEP DIDN'T SEEM TO WANT MY COIN UPSTAIRS...

JINGLE

...BUT IF YOU'D BE SO KIND AS TO PASS THIS ALONG, IT SHOULD MORE THAN COVER OUR REVELRY HERE.

WAIT--

GRIT
CREATIVE TEAM

RIAN WICKMAN is a comic writer and public librarian living in Baltimore, Maryland. He is the co-creator of the comics GRIT and BIG WHITE.

EVIN CASTANIERO is a freelance illustrator hailing from sunny California, where he spends most of his time drawing ntestines and petting his two cats.

IMON GOUGH is a comic book colourist from the UK, ailing from Birmingham, in the Midlands. He has worked on roperties such as G.I Joe, TMNT, Ringside, and the Aliens/ redator franchises.

ICAH MYERS is a comic book letterer from Portsmouth, irginia. He has lettered comics for Image, Dark Horse, DW, Scout, Starburns, Heavy Metal, Mad Cave, Devil's Due, nd many more.

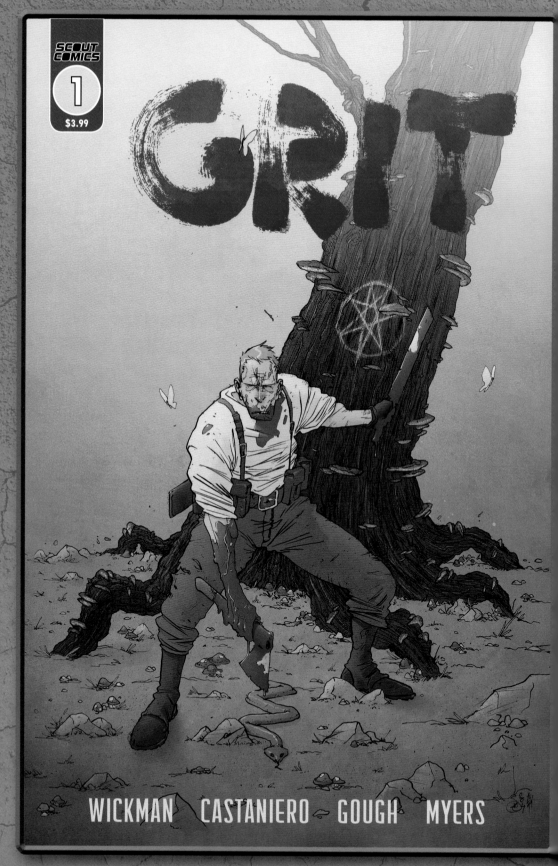

SCOUT COMICS

1

$3.99

GRIT

WICKMAN ╱ CASTANIERO ╱ GOUGH ╱ MYERS

Standard
Cover

-ISSUE ONE-

Kevin
Castaniero

Space Cadets
Exclusive

-ISSUE ONE-

Kevin
Castaniero

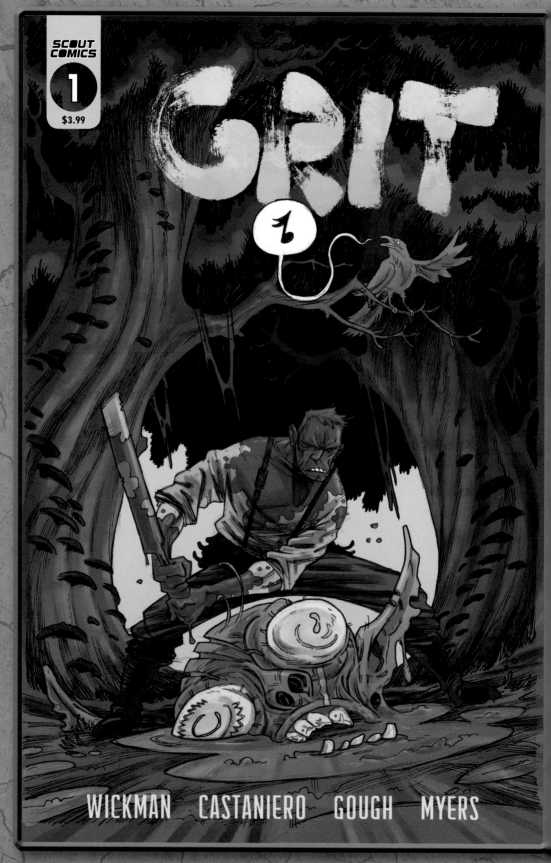

SCOUT COMICS

1
VARIANT

GRIT

WICKMAN   CASTANIERO   GOUGH   MYERS

-ISSUE ONE-   Artyom
TraKhanov

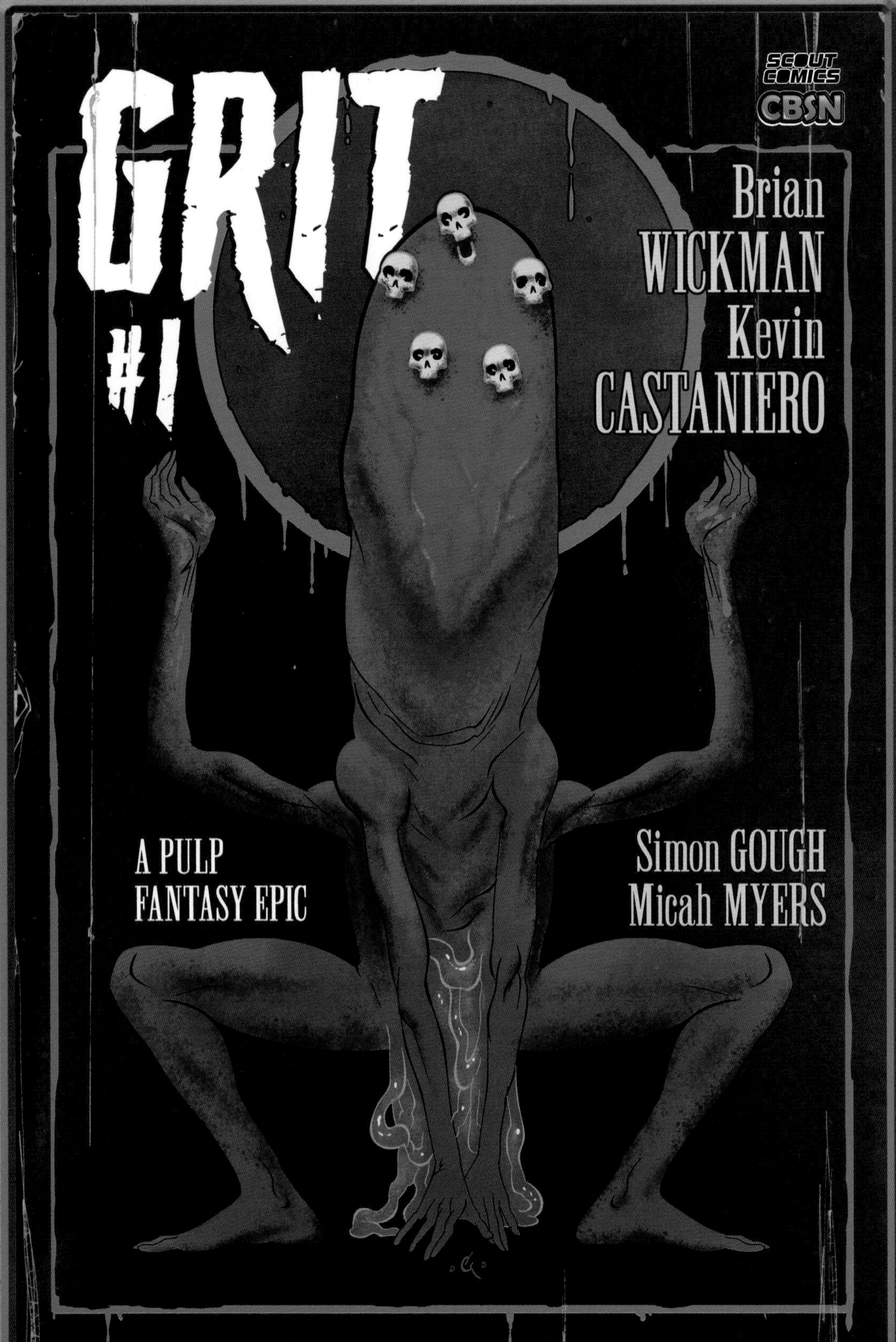

CBSN Variant

-ISSUE ONE-

Goran Gligović

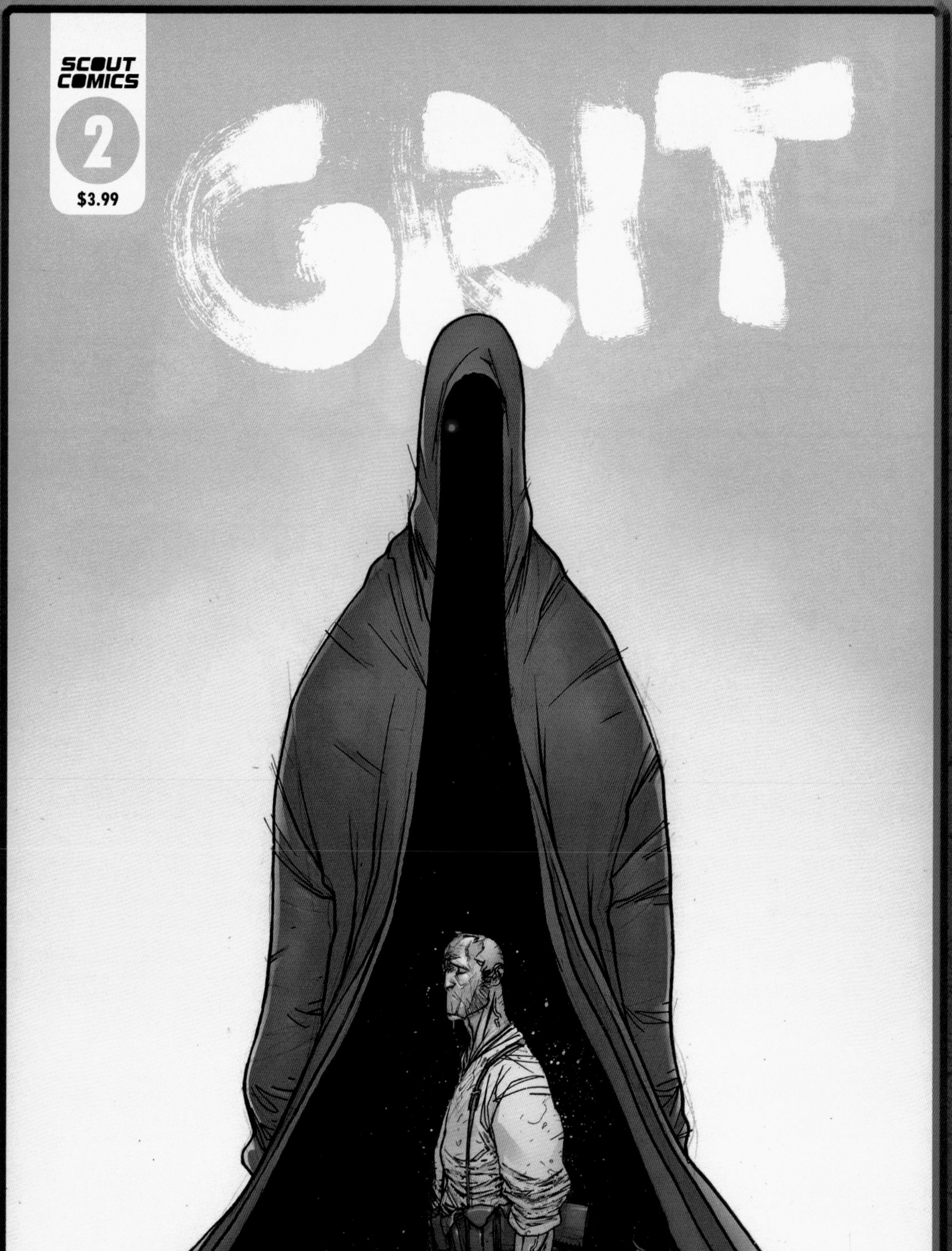

Standard Cover -ISSUE TWO- Kevin Castaniero

SCOUT COMICS

2

VARIANT

GRIT

THE SOUND OF BARROW

LOST IN THE BOG

IN THE CULT'S CLUTCHES NOW

MR. CURMUDGEONLY

BY THE OLD FISHING HOLE BACK HOME

ARI'S GONE

I'M FREE FROM THE GOBLIN GANG NOW

IF I WERE A MONSTER HUNTER

A REVENANT NAMED ANDRE

FORTY SHADES OF RED

ONE LIMB AT A TIME

DON'T TAKE YOUR AXE TO TOWN

BLACK DOG BOTTOM BLUES

WICKMAN CASTANIERO GOUGH MYERS

Scout Webstore

-ISSUE TWO-

Ally Cat

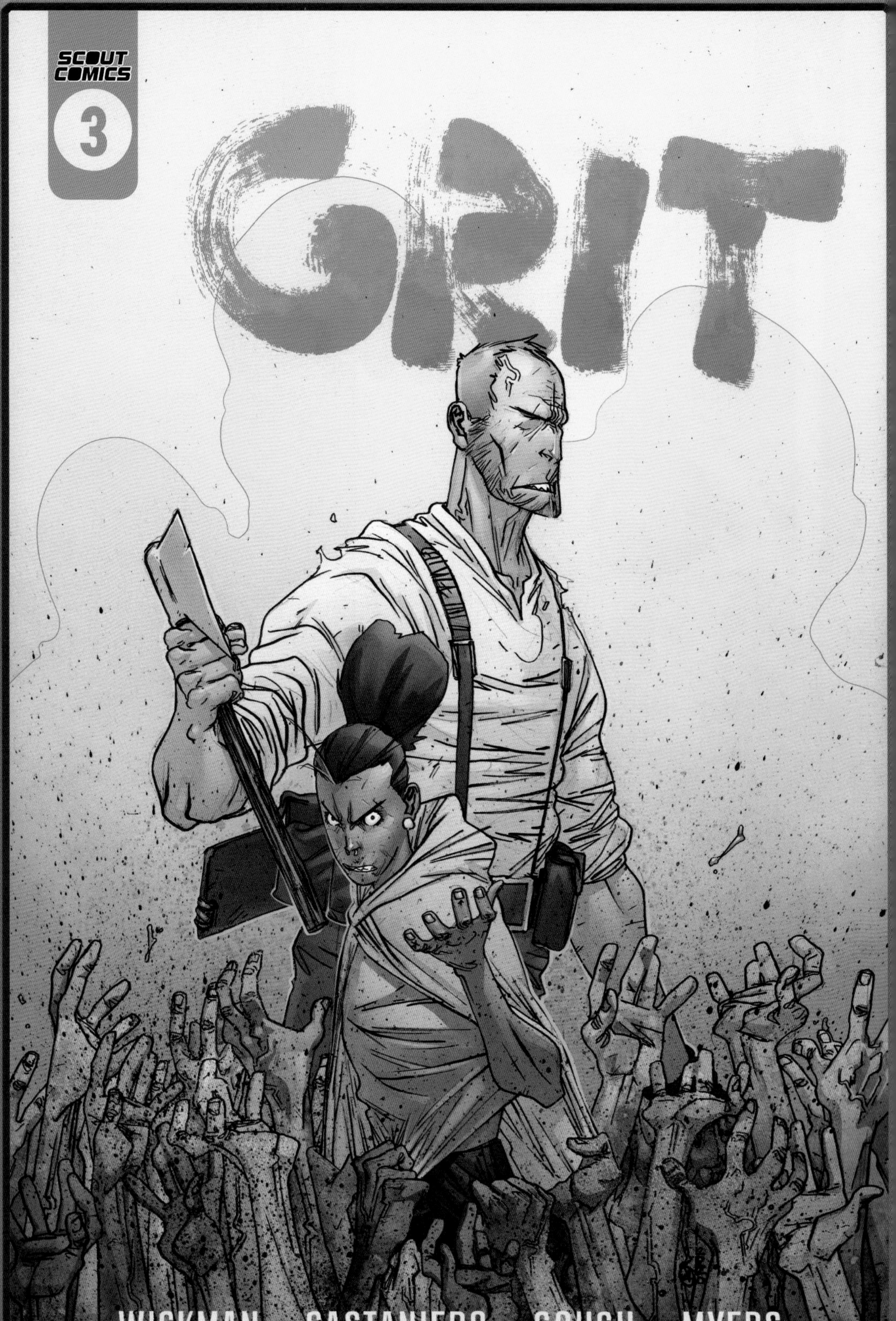

Standard Cover

-ISSUE THREE-

Kevin Castaniero